First published
by Kitchen Press Ltd,
1 Windsor Place, Dundee DD2 1BG
www.kitchenpress.co.uk

Text © Fraser Reid

Illustrations © Jen Collins
www.hellojenuine.com

Designed and typeset by Stuart Cockburn
www.stuartcockburn.com

A CIP catalogue record for this book
is available from the British Library.

ISBN: 978-0-9570373-5-9

Printed and bound in Scotland
by Martins the Printers Ltd

ACKNOWLEDGEMENTS

I would like to thank the customers of Fraser's Fruit & Veg – without them the shop wouldn't exist and wouldn't be so much fun. All members of the Fraser's Fruit & Veg team absolutely love opening our doors each morning and coming into work (even when it's – 4°). Also, my publisher Emily for maintaining focus and pushing me to get this book finished; it's been a long time coming and as I procrastinate over writing these acknowledgements I know she will keep me on page, so to speak. I would like to thank Jen Collins who is a fantastic illustrator and friend; she truly doesn't know how good she is and drew lots of lovely pictures of fruits and vegetables for me many years ago and probably thought I'd never get round to using them. I thank her for both her skill and her patience. Thanks also to designer Stuart Cockburn for making this book look so good. I would like to thank my soup guinea-pig Paula, she puts up with the mess I make in the kitchen and is forced to try all of the weird and wonderful soups that exist in my head. Her brutal honesty and hatred of woody herbs make soup creating both challenging and enjoyable. Finally I would like to thank my friends and family for their support in not only writing this book but helping me to achieve a life where you look forward to waking up every day and chatting to people about food. It is my passion; it's why I started the shop and there's nothing else I'd rather be doing every day.

Lastly I would like to thank my trusty wooden spoon. It's helped to make every single soup we've ever put out and is still going strong four years later.

Contents

INTRODUCTION

Who would have thought the nostalgic taste of a pea pod could create a cook book? My journey as a greengrocer started in the summer of 2009 when I came across a thriving village shop in Northern Ireland packed with local, seasonal produce. The owner gave us some of their fresh peas to try, something I hadn't eaten since I was a kid, and I started to think – where could I find a shop like this in my hometown? Incredibly, at that point, there were no dedicated greengrocers shops in the whole of Dundee, so I decided to open one. Three months later Fraser's Fruit & Veg opened its door in the heart of Dundee's West End.

Our premise was to provide our customers with as much fresh and local produce as we could get. Dundee is incredibly lucky to be surrounded by great farming lands with a massive variety of fresh produce and we even buy produce from local allotments and gardens. That's the key really: to get produce harvested that morning and onto the shelves within the next couple of hours. We love being a bustling shop and meeting place for the local community, and we're quite often asked to get in a coffee machine so people can have a seat and chat with other shoppers.

The idea of soup bags came about with the help of Jan McTaggart, now the co-owner of another beautiful greengrocers, Clementine of Broughty Ferry. In our former life as art centre marketeers, we used to talk about our dream local shop, how it could create recipes for soup and supply customers with everything they needed to make it, encouraging them to try out new flavours and ingredients and making it easy to cook at home. We've both gone our own ways with the concept and Clementine continue to motivate and excite me with their wonderful creations.

Our first soup bag was a very simple Lentil, and as the weeks and years went by our recipes became more creative, elaborate and damn tasty. I'm not a trained cook but I just like to experiment and try out new flavours; I'm constantly thinking – could that meal I just ate be turned into a soup? It's great fun and we try and keep our recipes as simple as possible so people don't have to go searching for obscure ingredients. The soup bags were a hit from day one, and even more fulfilling than seeing a new generation of novice cooks buying them was seeing people who have been making soup for 50 years trying them out. We had one customer who had been married for 57 years and had never cooked for his wife but every Tuesday he would come in and buy a soup bag and cook it for her. Soup is simple!

This book brings together 52 of our favourite vegetarian recipes with tips and variations to inspire you to make soup for every season. From Alternative Scotch Broth to Persian Root & Fruit, it's your seasonal guide and soup bible for simple, healthy and cost-effective meals.

We hope you enjoy making these soups as much as we've enjoyed creating them.

Fraser

A WORD ON STOCK

I hate to say it, but I think it's almost completely pointless making your own vegetable stock – essentially, a soup – to make vegetable soup. I always use good quality vegetable stock cubes, crumbled into the pan along with boiling water to save on washing up – though if you prefer to make up the stock before pouring it in, go right ahead. If you're not a veggie and you have some home-made chicken stock, use the same amounts as specified of boiling water; it will always add a lovely depth of flavour.

January

You would think that January is a drab and cold month where everyone is trying to get back into a healthy routine after the excesses of Christmas and Hogmanay, but let me tell you, it's amazing for a fruit and veg shop. Everyone is trying to get their five-a-day, and what better way to do this than by having soup for lunch or dinner? January also has some amazing ingredients bang in season. Citrus fruit is as good as it gets with Seville oranges and the sweetest clementines. In the veg world, there's nothing better than some turnip on Burns Night or using super sweet carrots and parsnips and balancing them with spices and fruits in soups and casseroles.

WINTER SPICED CARROT

This is a lovely, warming soup with caraway seeds giving an unusual aromatic twist. Some toasted mixed nuts would be a wonderful garnish.

OLIVE OIL OR BUTTER	1 tablespoon
ONION	1, peeled and roughly chopped
GARLIC	2 cloves, peeled and finely chopped
CARROTS	800g, peeled and roughly chopped
FRESH GINGER	2cm, peeled and grated
CARAWAY SEEDS	1 teaspoon
GRATED NUTMEG	pinch
STOCK CUBES	2
SALT AND FRESHLY GROUND BLACK PEPPER	to taste

Serves 4

Heat a pot on a medium heat and add the oil or butter. When it's hot, add the onion and garlic and fry on a low heat for 5–10 minutes, until they soften slightly.

Put in the carrot, ginger, caraway seeds and nutmeg and give everything a stir.

Pour in 1.2 litres of boiling water, then crumble in the stock cubes, turn up the heat and bring everything to the boil.

Turn down the heat and simmer the soup for 30 minutes.

Blend it until smooth and season to taste with salt and pepper.

SPICY KALE & NOODLE

This is always a popular soup at the beginning of the year: it's lightning quick, tasty and healthy. Some of our customers turn it into a main meal by adding some leftover chicken or prawns. Add a dash of soy sauce instead of salt to season as it'll give the broth a nice dark colour.

SUNFLOWER OIL	1 tablespoon
FRESH GINGER	thumb-sized piece, peeled and very finely chopped
GARLIC	2 cloves, peeled and very finely chopped
CHILLI	1, finely chopped
CARROT	1, peeled and very finely chopped
GROUND CORIANDER	1 teaspoon
STOCK CUBES	2
CURLY KALE	100g, leaves picked off and very finely sliced
DRIED EGG OR RICE NOODLES	1 nest
SPRING ONION	1, finely sliced

Serves 4

Put the oil in a large pot and fry the ginger, garlic, chilli, carrot and ground coriander on a low heat for 5 minutes or so until soft and fragrant.

Pour in 1.6 litres of boiling water and add the crumbled stock cubes, then the kale and the noodles.

Bring to the boil and simmer for 5 minutes until the noodles are cooked and the kale is tender.

Garnish with the sliced spring onion and serve.

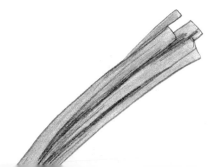

PERSIAN ROOT & FRUIT

This is the kind of flavour that I love: the sweetness from the root veg and pear balances well with the aromatic spices. This spice mix is great with any root veg soup.

OLIVE OIL OR BUTTER	I tablespoon
ONION	I, peeled and roughly chopped
GARLIC	2 cloves, peeled and finely chopped
PAPRIKA	I teaspoon
CORIANDER SEEDS	I teaspoon
CUMIN SEEDS	I teaspoon
CARROTS	2, peeled and roughly chopped
PARSNIP	I, peeled and roughly chopped
TURNIP	300g piece, peeled and roughly chopped
PEAR	I, peeled, cored and roughly chopped
STOCK CUBES	2
SALT AND FRESHLY GROUND BLACK PEPPER	to taste

Serves 4

Heat a pot on a medium-low heat and add the oil or butter. Fry the onion and garlic for 5–10 minutes until soft.

Toast the paprika, coriander and cumin seeds in a dry frying pan over a medium heat for a minute or two – they are ready when they start to release their smell.

Add the spices to the softened onion and garlic, and then stir in the carrots, parsnip, turnip and pear and give everything a mix.

Pour in 1.2 litres of boiling water and crumble in the stock cubes. Bring everything to the boil. Reduce the heat and simmer for 25 minutes.

Season the soup well to taste and blitz until smooth.

GOLDEN CAULIFLOWER & ALMOND

The Spanish love to use cauliflower and almond together, and giving it a twist of golden turmeric and carrot turns this soup into something altogether different and incredibly tasty.

OLIVE OIL OR BUTTER	1 tablespoon
ONION	1, peeled and finely chopped
CARROTS	2 medium, peeled and roughly chopped
GARLIC	2 cloves, peeled and finely chopped
GROUND ALMONDS	60g
CAULIFLOWER	1, leaves removed, roughly chopped
GROUND TURMERIC	1 teaspoon
STOCK CUBES	2
SALT AND FRESHLY GROUND BLACK PEPPER	to taste

Serves 4

Heat a pot on a medium-low heat and add the oil or butter. When it's hot, add the onion, carrots and garlic and fry for 5–10 minutes until they soften slightly.

Put in the ground almonds, cauliflower and turmeric and give everything a stir.

Pour in 1.2 litres of boiling water, then crumble the stock cubes into the pot and bring everything to the boil. Turn down the heat and simmer it for 20 minutes.

Blend the soup until smooth and season to taste with salt and freshly ground black pepper.

RABBIE BURNS

We had fun with this play on words, and the soup makes a nice starter on Burns Night. The pepper adds a touch of sweetness but is mostly there to add colour: we found out quickly that people are picky about the colour of their soups! For a milder flavour, deseed the chilli before you chop it.

OLIVE OIL OR BUTTER	1 tablespoon
ONION	1, peeled and roughly chopped
CHILLI	1, finely chopped
RED PEPPER	1, deseeded and roughly chopped
SWEDE	750g, peeled and roughly chopped
STOCK CUBES	2
SALT AND FRESHLY GROUND BLACK PEPPER	to taste

Serves 4

Heat a pot on a medium-low heat and add the tablespoon of oil or butter. Fry the onions, chilli and red pepper for 5–10 minutes, until everything is soft but not browned.

Stir in the swede, and then add the stock cubes dissolved in 1.2 litres of boiling water.

Bring everything to the boil and then simmer for 30 minutes until the swede is absolutely tender.

Blend the soup until smooth and season with salt and plenty of freshly ground black pepper.

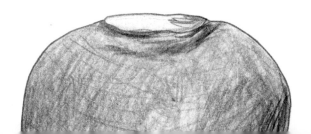

February

February, the shortest month of the year, is the gateway to spring. It can either feel like the depths of winter or you can start to look forward to better days. It's a little bit of an inbetween month for fruit and veg too, but Sicilian blood oranges – which are a personal favourite – hit the shelves in Feb and the shop is full of local root veg, Brussels sprouts and cabbages.

SPANISH SPLIT PEA

This soup was inspired by the classic pea and ham but as usual we gave it a little twist. I started out making a soup with chorizo and split pea (very nice if you feel like trying it out) but decided to make it vegetarian by adding extra garlic, some smoked paprika and celery for a little more peppery depth. This is an easy one to make out of store cupboard ingredients, a bit of limp celery from the bottom of the fridge and a spare onion. The split peas do not need to be soaked beforehand.

OLIVE OIL OR BUTTER	I tablespoon
ONION	I, peeled and diced
CELERY	I stick, diced
CARROT	I, peeled and diced
GARLIC	2 cloves, peeled and finely chopped
GREEN OR YELLOW SPLIT PEES	350g, rinsed
SMOKED PAPRIKA	I teaspoon
STOCK CUBE	I
SALT AND FRESHLY GROUND BLACK PEPPER	to taste

Serves 4

Put the oil or butter in a pot over a medium-low heat, then add the onion, vegetables and garlic and fry gently for 5–10 minutes, until they are soft.

Add the split peas and smoked paprika and give everything a stir.

Pour in 2 litres of boiling water, crumble in the stock cube, and then turn up the heat and boil hard for 5 minutes. Reduce the heat, cover and simmer for 45–50 minutes, keeping a close eye on it for the last 10 minutes to make sure it doesn't get too thick. (If it does, add a splash of boiling water.)

Blend the soup 'til smooth and season with salt and freshly ground black pepper.

LEEK, POTATO & ROASTED GARLIC

Our take on the classic soup — it's astounding that four ingredients can create such a wonderful and comforting soup.

GARLIC	I bulb, unpeeled
OLIVE OIL OR BUTTER	I tablespoon
LEEK	I large, washed and finely sliced
POTATOES	500g, peeled and diced into 2cm cubes
STOCK CUBES	2
SALT AND FRESHLY GROUND BLACK PEPPER	to taste

Serves 4

Preheat your oven to 190°C. Put the whole garlic bulb on a baking tray and bake for 30 minutes.

Meanwhile, heat the oil or butter in a pot and fry the leek on a low heat for 5–10 minutes.

Add the potatoes and give everything a stir.

Pour in 1.2 litres of boiling water and crumble in the stock cubes. Bring to the boil, and then turn the heat to low and simmer for 20 minutes.

When the garlic is done, squeeze the soft, sweet cloves out of their skin and add them to the soup. Blend everything 'til smooth and season to taste with salt and plenty of freshly ground black pepper.

SWEET POTATO, LENTIL & BLOOD ORANGE

This is a lovely sweet and zesty soup: it can be made with ordinary oranges but it's a great excuse to use sweet Sicilian blood oranges which are in the shop from December to March.

OLIVE OIL OR BUTTER	1 tablespoon
ONION	1, peeled and roughly chopped
GARLIC	2 cloves, peeled and finely chopped
SWEET POTATO	1 small, peeled and roughly chopped
CARROT	1, peeled and roughly chopped
RED LENTILS	175g, rinsed well
STOCK CUBES	2
BLOOD ORANGE	juice and zest of 1
SALT AND FRESHLY GROUND BLACK PEPPER	to taste

Serves 4

Put a pot on a medium-low heat and add the oil or butter. When it's hot, fry the onion and garlic for 5–10 minutes until they're soft.

Add the sweet potato, carrot and lentils and give everything a stir.

Pour in 1.2 litres of boiling water, and crumble in the stock cubes along with the juice and zest of the orange. Bring everything to the boil, and then turn down the heat and simmer for 20 minutes.

Season the soup to taste with salt and freshly ground black pepper and blend until smooth.

CURRIED PARSNIP

Everyone loves curried parsnip soup; it's so simple to make and so tasty. It's really easy to vary too: just change up the spices – any mix of mild and aromatic spices like cumin, coriander, turmeric and paprika work well. Sometimes I add a teaspoon of honey to help bring out the natural sweetness of the parsnips.

OLIVE OIL OR BUTTER	1 tablespoon
ONION	1, peeled and diced
GARLIC	2 cloves, peeled and finely chopped
MILD CURRY POWDER	1 teaspoon
CORIANDER SEEDS	1 teaspoon
GROUND GINGER	½ teaspoon
PARSNIP	750g, peeled and roughly chopped
STOCK CUBES	2
SALT AND FRESHLY GROUND BLACK PEPPER	to taste

Serves 4

Heat the oil or butter in a pot, then add the onions and garlic and fry everything on a medium-low heat for 5–10 minutes.

Meanwhile, put the spices into a dry frying pan over a medium heat and toast them until they start to release their fragrance (about 2–3 minutes).

Add the toasted spices and the chopped parsnips to the softened onions and give everything a mix.

Pour in 1.2 litres of boiling water, crumble in the stock cubes and bring it all to the boil.

Reduce the heat and simmer for 20–25 minutes.

Blend the soup until smooth and season with salt and plenty of freshly ground black pepper.

March

We hate March in the shop – it's a little bit too late for the winter veg and the spring and summer stuff is just being planted in the ground. We are desperate to see the start of the spring produce so have to be creative with our soup ingredients and head to the store cupboard to keep things exciting.

ALTERNATIVE SCOTCH BROTH

This is a nice introduction to the ugly root vegetable celeriac. It has a peppery taste and a creamy texture and balances really well with woody herbs. In this soup we use it with carrots, leeks and barley, but feel free to use any mixture of different root vegetables.

OLIVE OIL OR BUTTER	1 tablespoon
LEEK	1 medium, washed and finely chopped
CARROTS	2, peeled and diced
CELERIAC	½, trimmed and diced
PEARL BARLEY	100g, rinsed
STOCK CUBES	2
SALT AND FRESHLY GROUND BLACK PEPPER	to taste

Serves 4

Heat a pot on a medium heat and add the oil or butter. Fry the leek for 5–10 minutes, until it's soft but not coloured.

Add the carrot, celeriac and barley to the pot and continue to fry for 2 minutes, giving everything a mix while you go.

Pour in 1.5 litres of boiling water, crumble in the stock cubes then bring everything to the boil. Turn down the heat and simmer gently for 25 minutes.

Season the soup well to taste – lots of freshly ground black pepper is good here.

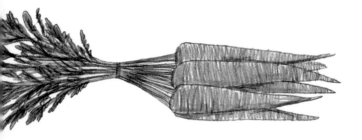

CHILLI PEPPER CHICKPEA

Try saying that quickly three times! A great warming but fresh soup; you can eat it chunky, but if you blend it then you will really taste the nutty flavour of the chickpeas.

OLIVE OIL OR BUTTER	1 tablespoon
RED ONION	1, peeled and roughly chopped
GARLIC	2 cloves, peeled and finely chopped
CHILLI	1, deseeded (optional) and finely chopped
CARROTS	3, peeled and roughly chopped
RED PEPPER	1, deseeded and roughly chopped
CHICK PEAS	1 x 400g tin, drained
STOCK CUBES	2
SALT AND FRESHLY GROUND BLACK PEPPER	to taste

Serves 4

Heat a pot on a medium heat and add the oil or butter. Fry all of the vegetables for 10 minutes until soft but not coloured.

Stir in the drained chickpeas, give it all a good mix, and then add 1.2 litres of boiling water and the crumbled stock cubes. Bring to the boil and then lower the heat and simmer for 20 minutes.

Season the soup to taste and either serve as it is or put in the blender and blitz until smooth.

GRANNY SMITH GREEN

Named after the famous bright green apple, this soup oozes healthiness and is a fantastic blend of leafy greens, silky smooth courgettes and cashew. This soup could be changed really easily by substituting basil or parsley for the coriander.

OLIVE OIL OR BUTTER	1 tablespoon
ONION	1, peeled and roughly chopped
GARLIC	2 cloves, peeled and finely chopped
CARROT	1 large, peeled and roughly chopped
COURGETTE	1 large, roughly chopped
UNSALTED CASHEW NUTS	50g
FRESH CORIANDER	1 bunch, finely chopped
STOCK CUBES	2
SPINACH	250g, washed
SALT AND FRESHLY GROUND BLACK PEPPER	to taste

Serves 4

Heat the olive oil or butter in a pot over a medium-low heat. Fry the onion and garlic for 5–10 minutes until they soften slightly.

Add the carrot, courgette, cashews and fresh coriander to the pot, mixing everything together.

Pour in a litre of boiling water, crumble in the stock cubes and bring it all to the boil. Turn down the heat and simmer for 20 minutes.

Take the pot off the heat and stir in the spinach until it wilts.

Blend the soup for at least 3 minutes to get a really silky smooth finish. Season it to taste.

SMOKY SWEET POTATO & BUTTERBEAN

Hands down this is one of my favourite soup recipes and it always goes down well with customers. The creamy butterbeans are the perfect balance for the smoky paprika and sweetness of the potatoes.

OLIVE OIL OR BUTTER	1 tablespoon
ONION	1, peeled and roughly chopped
GARLIC	2 cloves, peeled and finely chopped
SWEET POTATO	1, peeled and roughly chopped
CARROTS	1 or 2, peeled and roughly chopped
BUTTERBEANS	1 x 400g tin, drained
SMOKED PAPRIKA	1 teaspoon
STOCK CUBES	2
SALT AND FRESHLY GROUND BLACK PEPPER	to taste

Serves 4

Heat a pot on a medium heat and add the oil or butter. Fry the onion and garlic for 5–10 minutes until they soften slightly.

Add the sweet potato, carrots, drained butterbeans and smoked paprika to the pot, mixing everything together.

Pour in 1.2 litres of boiling water, crumble in the stock cubes, and then bring it all to the boil. Turn down the heat and simmer for 20 minutes.

Blend the soup and season to taste.

SPICY (OR NOT) TOMATO & LENTIL

The chilli is optional here – the soup is great either way. If you do want some heat, why not try a Kashmiri or chipotle chilli to vary the flavour.

OLIVE OIL OR BUTTER	1 tablespoon
ONION	1, peeled and roughly chopped
GARLIC	2 cloves, peeled and finely chopped
TOMATOES	1 x 400g tin
FRESH GINGER	2cm, peeled and finely chopped
GROUND CUMIN	1 teaspoon
CHILLI	1, deseeded (optional) and finely chopped
RED LENTILS	175g, rinsed
STOCK CUBE	1
SALT AND FRESHLY GROUND BLACK PEPPER	to taste

Serves 4

Heat the olive oil or butter in a pot on a medium-low heat. Fry the onion and garlic for 5–10 minutes until soft.

Add the tomatoes, ginger, ground cumin, half of the chilli and the lentils and give everything a stir.

Pour in 1.2 litres of boiling water, crumble in the stock cube and bring everything to the boil. Turn down the heat and simmer for 30 minutes.

Blend the soup and season well. Add a little more chopped chilli to each bowl according to taste.

April

This is the start of the new season produce coming in: some early British asparagus, spinach and look out for the slim pink stems of Yorkshire rhubarb. This rhubarb, although fairly pricey, is the sign that the warmer temperatures are on their way. Its tender and tangy flavour will help lift a rich dessert – maybe not so great for soup though.

GOLDEN DAHL & SPINACH

This makes a fantastic soup, but you could also easily turn it into a side or main dish by simmering for longer until you get a thicker consistency. The split peas do not need to be soaked beforehand.

OLIVE OIL OR BUTTER	I tablespoon
ONION	I, peeled and finely chopped
GARLIC	2 cloves, peeled and finely chopped
FRESH GINGER	2cm, peeled and finely chopped
CHILLI	I, deseeded (optional) and finely chopped
YELLOW SPLIT PEAS	350g, rinsed
GROUND TURMERIC	I teaspoon
GROUND CORIANDER	I teaspoon
STOCK CUBES	2
SPINACH	250g, washed
FRESH CORIANDER	a handful, finely chopped
SALT AND FRESHLY GROUND BLACK PEPPER	to taste

Serves 4

Heat a pot on a medium-low heat and add the oil or butter. Fry the onion, garlic, ginger and chilli 5–10 minutes until soft and fragrant.

Add the split peas, turmeric and ground coriander and give everything a stir.

Pour in 1.5 litres of boiling water, crumble in the stock cubes, and then bring the pot to the boil. Turn down the heat and simmer for 45–50 minutes.

Remove the pot from the heat and add the spinach, stirring until it has wilted. Finish with the chopped coriander and serve.

ROASTED PEPPER, LENTIL & THYME

Our neighbours at EspressOh! think this is one of our best soups and quite often have it for sale in their café. It's always a firm favourite with our younger customers as it's got a great consistency and sweet flavour.

RED PEPPERS	2, deseeded and quartered
OLIVE OIL OR BUTTER	1 tablespoon
ONION	1, peeled and roughly chopped
GARLIC	2 cloves, peeled and finely chopped
RED LENTILS	200g, rinsed well
FRESH THYME	a few sprigs, leaves only
STOCK CUBES	2
SALT AND FRESHLY GROUND BLACK PEPPER	to taste

Serves 4

Preheat the oven to 190°C. Put your quartered peppers on a baking tray and roast for 20 minutes.

Meanwhile, put the oil or butter in a pot over a medium-low heat and fry the onion and garlic for 5–10 minutes until they are soft.

Take the peppers out of the oven and, if you like, remove their blackened skin – it's up to you. I never bother. Add them to the pan along with the lentils and thyme leaves and give everything a good stir.

Pour in 1.4 litres of boiling water, crumble in the stock cubes, and then bring it all to the boil. Turn down the heat and simmer for 15–20 minutes.

Blend the soup and season to taste.

BOMBAY POTATO

To make a really nice Indian side dish, just leave out the stock. Simply cover and simmer the dish on a low heat for about 10 minutes after you've added tomatoes.

OLIVE OIL OR BUTTER	1 tablespoon
ONION	1, peeled and diced
FRESH GINGER	2cm, peeled and grated
SMALL AND WAXY POTATOES	500g, roughly chopped
GARAM MASALA	1 teaspoon
GROUND CORIANDER	1 teaspoon
TURMERIC	1 teaspoon
BLACK MUSTARD SEEDS	1 teaspoon
GROUND CUMIN	½ teaspoon
TOMATOES	3, roughly chopped
STOCK CUBES	2
SALT AND FRESHLY GROUND BLACK PEPPER	to taste

Serves 4

Heat a pot on a medium-low heat and add the oil or butter. Fry the onion, ginger, potatoes and spices for 10 minutes, stirring to make sure the spices coat everything.

Add the tomatoes, stir, and then pour in 1.2 litres of boiling water and crumble in the stock cubes. Bring to the boil, then turn down the heat and simmer it for 20 minutes.

Season the soup to taste and serve either as it is or blended – it's up to you.

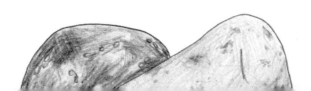

SMOKED CHIPOTLE CHILLI BEAN

This soup is delicious garnished with a handful of tortilla chips and a dollop of sour cream or crème fraîche.

OLIVE OIL OR BUTTER	1 tablespoon
ONION	1, peeled and diced
GARLIC	2 cloves, peeled and finely chopped
NEW POTATOES	8, diced into 1–2cm cubes
TOMATOES	5, quartered
DRIED CHIPOTLE CHILLI	1
SMOKED PAPRIKA	1 teaspoon
MIXED BEANS	1 x 400g tin, drained
STOCK CUBES	2
SALT AND FRESHLY GROUND BLACK PEPPER	to taste

Serves 4

Heat a pot on a medium heat and add the oil or butter. Fry the onion and garlic for 5–10 minutes until soft.

Add the potatoes, tomatoes, whole chipotle chilli, smoked paprika and drained beans and give it a good mix.

Pour in 1.2 litres of boiling water, crumble in the stock cubes, and then bring the pot to the boil. Lower the heat and simmer for 20 minutes.

Take out the whole chilli. If you like things hot, cut off the chilli stalk, then chop the rest of it up and stir it back into the soup. If not, just discard it. Season the soup and serve.

May

May sees the beginning of a steady stream of local produce coming into the shop. The local farmers offer purple sprouting broccoli, spring cabbages, rhubarb and mixture of freshly cut herbs.

ASIAN NOODLE BROTH

Use any kind of spring cabbage that's not very tightly packed for this one.

SUNFLOWER OIL	I tablespoon
CARROT	I, peeled and very finely chopped
FRESH GINGER	thumb-sized piece, peeled and very finely chopped
GARLIC	2 cloves, peeled and crushed
CHILLI	I, deseeded (optional) and finely chopped
LEAFY CABBAGE	¼, very finely shredded
STOCK CUBES	2
DRIED NOODLES	2 nests
SPRING ONION	I, finely chopped

Serves 4

Heat the oil in a pot over a medium-low heat, and fry the carrot, ginger, garlic and chilli for 5–10 minutes until soft.

Stir in the cabbage, and then pour in 1.6 litres of boiling water. Crumble in the stock cubes, add the noodles and then bring it to the boil and simmer for 5 minutes or until the noodles are cooked.

Garnish the soup with the chopped spring onions, and feel free to add a couple of dashes of soy sauce or sesame oil to finish it off.

GREEN LENTIL & MIXED HERB

Equally as delicious if you use thyme or sage or really any mixture of woody herbs – experiment!

OLIVE OIL OR BUTTER	I tablespoon
RED ONION	I, peeled and roughly chopped
LEEK	I, washed well and finely chopped
CELERY	2 sticks, finely chopped
ROSEMARY	I sprig, leaves removed and finely chopped
CARROTS	3, peeled and diced into I–2 cm cubes
GREEN LENTILS	175g, rinsed
FRESH BAY LEAVES	2 (dried are fine if you can't get hold of fresh ones)
STOCK CUBES	2
SALT AND FRESHLY GROUND BLACK PEPPER	to taste

Serves 4

Heat a pot on a medium-low heat and add the oil or butter. Fry the onion, leek, celery and rosemary for 5–10 minutes until they soften.

Add the carrots, lentils and bay leaves, giving everything a stir.

Pour in 1.2 litres of boiling water, crumble in the stock cubes and bring everything to the boil. Turn down the heat and simmer for 30 minutes.

Remove the bay leaves before eating and season the soup well.

ITALIAN WHITE BEAN
& CHERRY TOMATO

If you can find some fresh oregano or have some in the garden, then pick the leaves from a couple of sprigs instead of using dried oregano.

OLIVE OIL OR BUTTER	I tablespoon
ONION	I, peeled and finely chopped
CARROT	I, peeled and finely chopped
COURGETTE	I, finely chopped
GARLIC	2 cloves, peeled and finely chopped
CHERRY TOMATOES	10, halved
CANNELLINI BEANS	I x 400g tin, drained
DRIED OREGANO	I teaspoon
STOCK CUBES	2

Serves 4

Heat the oil or butter in a pot over a medium-low heat. Fry the onion, carrot, courgette and garlic for 5–10 minutes until they are soft.

Pop in the cherry tomatoes along with the beans and oregano and mix everything together.

Add a litre of boiling water and the crumbled stock cubes, and then bring everything to the boil. Turn down the heat and simmer for 15 minutes.

Try with a garnish of fresh basil on top.

CAJUN BLACK-EYED BEAN

I was making some gumbo one evening and thought – I could turn this into a soup. This is the easy version but if you can find any okra then a small handful wouldn't go amiss. This soup is really great garnished with a handful of tortilla chips to add some crunch.

OLIVE OIL OR BUTTER	1 tablespoon
ONION	1, peeled and diced into 1–2cm cubes
GREEN PEPPER	1, deseeded and diced into 2cm cubes
CELERY	2 sticks, finely sliced
GARLIC	2 cloves, peeled and finely chopped
TOMATOES	3, roughly chopped
BLACK-EYED BEANS	1 x 400g tin, drained
SMOKED PAPRIKA	1 teaspoon
CAYENNE PEPPER	a pinch
DRIED THYME	a pinch
STOCK CUBES	2
SALT AND FRESHLY GROUND BLACK PEPPER	to taste

Serves 4

Heat a pot on a medium-low heat and add the oil or butter. Fry the onions, green pepper, celery and garlic for 5–10 minutes until they soften.

Add the tomatoes to the pot along with the black-eyed beans and the spices and continue to cook for 5 minutes, stirring to stop anything sticking.

Pour in 1.2 litres of boiling water, crumble in the stock cubes, and then bring everything to the boil. Turn down the heat and simmer for 20–25 minutes.

Season to taste with salt and freshly ground black pepper.

June

What a month of fresh produce! It's the start of the local berries, fresh peas, beans and new potatoes. Also the Spanish stoned fruit season begins so grab as many peaches, nectarines and cherries as you can get your hands on... they're never better.

PEA & MINT

The classic summer soup – why try and change one of the best flavour matches in the world? If you can get a hold of apple mint then this gives the soup a different twist. You can use fresh podded peas, the same weight of frozen peas or make this in the winter with split peas. For the split pea option, use 350g split peas and add an extra 200ml of boiling water; then boil hard for 5 minutes and simmer for another 40.

OLIVE OIL OR BUTTER	1 tablespoon
ONION	1, peeled and diced
CELERY	1 stick, diced
CARROT	1, peeled and diced
GARLIC	2 cloves, peeled and finely chopped
PEAS	500g (podded weight)
FRESH MINT	a handful, finely chopped (or a teaspoon of dried)
STOCK CUBE	1
SALT AND FRESHLY GROUND BLACK PEPPER	to taste

Serves 4

Heat the oil or butter in a pot over a medium-low heat, then add the onion, celery, carrot and garlic and fry for 5–10 minutes until soft.

Stir in the peas and mint, and then add a litre of boiling water and the crumbled stock cube. Bring everything to the boil, and then turn down the heat and simmer for 15 minutes.

Season to taste and blend until smooth.

CHORBA BISSAR

This is an everyday soup in North Africa and makes great use of fresh broad beans. Out of season you can make it with dried broad beans, but you will need to simmer the soup for more like 40 minutes.

BROAD BEANS	1kg (unpodded weight)
OLIVE OIL OR BUTTER	1 tablespoon
ONION	1, peeled and roughly chopped
CARROT	1, peeled and roughly chopped
GARLIC	2 cloves, peeled and finely chopped
PAPRIKA	2 teaspoons
GROUND CUMIN	1 teaspoon
GARAM MASALA	1 teaspoon
STOCK CUBES	2
SALT AND FRESHLY GROUND BLACK PEPPER	to taste

Serves 4

Pod the broad beans.

Heat a pot on a medium-low heat and add the oil or butter. Fry the onion, carrot and garlic for 5–10 minutes until soft.

Stir in the podded broad beans and spices and give everything a mix.

Add 1.2 litres of boiling water and the crumbled stock cubes, and then bring the pot to the boil. Reduce the heat and simmer for 20 minutes.

Blitz the soup until smooth and season well to taste.

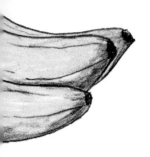

JAMAICAN CURRIED BANANA

Please trust us on this one – it's delicious! We like to serve it and let people guess what the ingredients are: they are so confused when you tell them it's banana soup. The Scotch bonnet chilli pepper is optional, but it gives a real Caribbean kick.

OLIVE OIL OR BUTTER	1 tablespoon
ONION	1, peeled and roughly chopped
GARLIC	2 cloves, peeled and finely chopped
CARROT	1, peeled and roughly chopped
SWEET POTATO	1, peeled and roughly chopped
CURRY POWDER	1½ teaspoons
BANANAS	2 (preferably greener ones), peeled and roughly chopped
STOCK CUBES	2
SCOTCH BONNET CHILLI PEPPER	1, whole (optional)
SALT AND FRESHLY GROUND BLACK PEPPER	to taste

Serves 4

Heat a pot on a medium-low heat and add the oil or butter. Add the onion and garlic and fry for 5–10 minutes until soft.

Stir in the carrot, sweet potato and curry powder, giving everything a mix, and then put in the chopped bananas.

Pour in 1.2 litres of boiling water along with the crumbled stock cubes and the whole Scotch bonnet. Bring everything to the boil and then simmer for 15–20 minutes.

Remove the chilli pepper before blending everything together, and then season the soup well to taste.

TOMATO & BASIL

This is a classic soup that can be enjoyed just as it is, but if you want to mix it up a little then try adding in some fresh mint and chilli. Or stir a swirl of crème fraîche into each bowl to make it nice and creamy.

OLIVE OIL OR BUTTER	1 tablespoon
ONION	1, peeled and roughly chopped
GARLIC	2 cloves, peeled and finely chopped
TOMATOES	750g, roughly chopped
STOCK CUBES	2
FRESH BASIL	a large handful
SALT AND FRESHLY GROUND BLACK PEPPER	to taste

Serves 4

Heat a pot on a medium-low heat and add the oil or butter. Fry the onion and garlic for 5–10 minutes until they soften slightly.

Turn up the heat a bit, add the tomatoes, and then cook for 10 minutes until they break down a bit.

Add 800ml boiling water and the crumbled stock cubes, and then bring everything to the boil and simmer for 15 minutes.

Tear the basil leaves off the stalks and pop them into the pot.

Blend everything together and season well with salt and freshly ground black pepper.

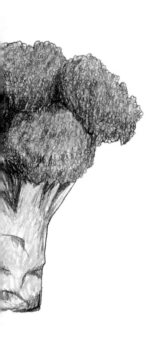

July

This is a great month whether you're growing vegetables in the garden or just shopping at your local greengrocer. Local brassicas like broccoli and cauliflower are in full flow, along with the new season baby carrots and beetroots. Also, if you're growing courgettes, then you should have a glut of them this month.

CHARLENE'S RUBY SOUP

This recipe comes from one of our suppliers at Scot-herbs. A luxurious ruby-coloured soup, it uses two kinds of fresh herbs which work wonderfully with the sweet beetroot and carrots.

OLIVE OIL OR BUTTER	1 tablespoon
ONION	1, peeled and roughly chopped
GARLIC	2 cloves, peeled and finely chopped
BEETROOT	2 tennis-ball-sized, peeled and diced into 2cm cubes
CARROTS	4 medium, peeled and diced into 2cm cubes
FRESH GINGER	thumb-sized piece, peeled and grated
FRESH CORIANDER	a small handful, finely chopped including the stalks
FRESH PARSLEY	a small handful, finely chopped including the stalks
STOCK CUBES	2
SALT AND FRESHLY GROUND BLACK PEPPER	to taste

Serves 4

Heat a pot on a medium-low heat and add the oil or butter. Fry the onion and garlic for 5–10 minutes, until soft.

Add the beetroot, carrots, ginger and herbs and give everything a mix.

Pour 1.2 litres of boiling water into the pot and crumble in the stock cubes. Bring everything to the boil and then reduce the heat and simmer with the lid on for 25–30 minutes.

Blend the soup until smooth and season well to taste.

PLUM TOMATO, ORZO & OREGANO

This is almost posh spaghetti hoops, possibly even quicker than opening the tin and heating them up too. It uses a small pasta grain called orzo – if you can't find this then risotto rice or 50g of small pasta would work. If you can find some fresh oregano then pick the leaves off a few sprigs instead of using dried.

OLIVE OIL OR BUTTER	1 tablespoon
ONION	1, peeled and diced into 2cm cubes
GARLIC	2 cloves, peeled and finely chopped
CARROT	1, peeled and diced into 2cm cubes
CELERY	1 stick, finely chopped
PLUM TOMATOES	5, roughly chopped
ORZO	100g
FRESH OREGANO	1 teaspoon, chopped (or 1 teaspoon dried)
STOCK CUBES	2
SALT AND FRESHLY GROUND BLACK PEPPER	to taste

Serves 4

Heat a pot on a medium heat and add the oil or butter. Fry the onion, garlic, carrot and celery for 5–10 minutes until they soften.

Add the roughly chopped tomatoes along with the orzo and oregano, and mix everything together.

Pour in 1.2 litres of boiling water, crumble in the stock cubes and bring to the boil. Then turn down the heat and simmer for 15 minutes.

Season to taste and feel free to garnish with some fresh basil on top.

CREAMY COURGETTE, CASHEW & MIXED HERB

This soup is light and incredibly smooth and creamy, and it can be enjoyed hot or chilled. It is also pretty cheap to make at this time of year. Any mixture of fresh herbs would work – try basil, parsley and oregano.

OLIVE OIL OR BUTTER	1 tablespoon
ONION	1, peeled and roughly chopped
GARLIC	2 cloves, peeled and finely chopped
CARROT	1 large, peeled and roughly chopped
COURGETTES	2 or 3, roughly chopped
UNSALTED CASHEW NUTS	50g
FRESH MIXED HERBS	a handful (or 1 teaspoon dried mixed herbs)
STOCK CUBES	2
SALT AND FRESHLY GROUND BLACK PEPPER	to taste

Serves 4

Heat the oil or butter in a pot on a medium-low heat. Fry the onion and garlic for 5–10 minutes until they are soft but not coloured.

Add the carrots, courgettes, cashews and mixed herbs to the pot, mixing everything together.

Pour in 1.2 litres of boiling water, crumble in the stock cubes and bring to the boil. Reduce the heat and simmer for 20 minutes.

Blend the soup for at least 3 minutes for a really silky smooth finish and season to taste.

BROC-A-LEEKIE

This is a fun veggie soup which can be handy when using up those wrinkly peppers or soft leeks at the end of the week.

OLIVE OIL OR BUTTER	1 tablespoon
LEEK	1, washed and finely chopped
RED OR GREEN PEPPER	1 small, deseeded and roughly chopped
GARLIC	2 cloves, peeled and finely chopped
BROCCOLI	1 head, roughly chopped (including the stalk)
POTATO	1 medium, peeled and roughly chopped
FRESH GINGER	2cm, peeled and grated
STOCK CUBES	2
SALT AND FRESHLY GROUND BLACK PEPPER	to taste

Serves 4

Heat a pot on a medium-low heat and add the oil or butter. Add the leek, pepper and garlic and then fry for 5–10 minutes until they soften.

Mix in the broccoli, potato and grated ginger and continue to cook for 2 minutes.

Pour in 1.2 litres of boiling water, crumble in the stock cubes and bring to the boil. Turn down the heat and simmer for 25 minutes.

Blend the soup 'til smooth and season to taste.

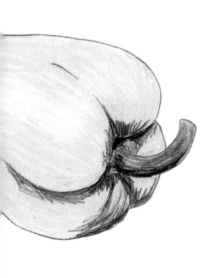

August

It's probably my favourite month for seasonal produce: you still have the lovely peaches, nectarines and apricots but glimpses of Autumn are on the way with the beginning of the British plum season. We also get loads of great local produce in, including chillies, peppers and fennel.

TOMATO, FENNEL & CAYENNE

These flavours work really well together and the fennel's aniseed taste mellows out when cooked.

OLIVE OIL OR BUTTER	1 tablespoon
FENNEL	1 bulb, finely chopped (set aside any leafy tops)
RED ONIONS	2, peeled and finely chopped
GARLIC	2 cloves, peeled and finely chopped
TOMATOES	500g, roughly chopped
CAYENNE PEPPER	½ teaspoon (or as much as you can handle)
STOCK CUBES	2
SALT AND FRESHLY GROUND BLACK PEPPER	to taste

Serves 4

Heat the olive oil or butter in a pot on a medium-low heat. Fry the fennel, onions and garlic for 10 minutes until they soften.

Add the tomatoes and cayenne pepper to the pot, mixing everything together.

Pour in 900ml of boiling water, chuck in the crumbled stock cubes and bring to the boil. Turn down the heat and simmer for 15–20 minutes.

Blend the soup and season to taste. Garnish each bowl with the chopped fennel tops.

CARROT, COURGETTE & CHILLI

This is one of our most popular soups; the courgettes make it silky smooth. Deseed the chilli if you don't like it too hot.

OLIVE OIL OR BUTTER	1 tablespoon
ONION	1, peeled and roughly chopped
GARLIC	2 cloves, peeled and finely chopped
CARROTS	4 or 5 medium, peeled and roughly chopped
COURGETTES	2, roughly chopped
CHILLI	1, finely chopped
STOCK CUBES	2
SALT AND FRESHLY GROUND BLACK PEPPER	to taste

Serves 4

Heat a pot on a medium-low heat and add the oil or butter. Fry the onion and garlic for 5–10 minutes.

Add the carrots, courgettes and chilli to the pot, mixing everything together.

Pour in 1.2 litres of boiling water and the crumbled stock cubes, turn up the heat and bring it to the boil. Reduce the heat and simmer for 20 minutes.

Blend the soup and season to taste.

SWEET SUMMER LENTIL

A fun summer soup which can be altered by swapping fresh nectarines or peaches for the apricots.

OLIVE OIL OR BUTTER	1 tablespoon
ONION	1, peeled and roughly chopped
GARLIC	2 cloves, peeled and finely chopped
CORIANDER SEEDS	1 teaspoon
CUMIN SEEDS	1 teaspoon
PLUM TOMATOES	3, roughly chopped
APRICOTS	3 or 4, destoned and roughly chopped (or 8 dried apricots, roughly chopped)
RED LENTILS	175g, washed well
STOCK CUBES	2
SALT AND FRESHLY GROUND BLACK PEPPER	to taste

Serves 4

Heat a pot on a medium-low heat and add a tablespoon of oil or butter. Fry the onion and garlic for 5–10 minutes until soft.

Meanwhile toast the spices in a dry frying pan for a few minutes until they start to release their smell. Stir them into the onions and garlic.

Add the roughly chopped tomatoes, apricots and lentils to the pot, and stir it all well.

Pour in 1.2 litres of boiling water, crumble in the stock cubes and bring to the boil. Reduce the heat and simmer for 20 minutes.

Season to taste and serve.

ROASTED PEPPER, BUTTERBEAN & ROSEMARY

You can give this a more Spanish flavour by adding a teaspoon of smoked paprika at the same time as the beans, peppers and rosemary.

RED PEPPERS	2, deseeded and quartered
OLIVE OIL	1½ tablespoons
ONION	1, peeled and roughly chopped
GARLIC	2 cloves, peeled and finely chopped
CARROTS	1 or 2, peeled and roughly chopped
BUTTERBEANS	1 x 400g tin, drained
ROSEMARY	1 sprig, leaves picked and finely chopped
STOCK CUBES	2
SALT AND FRESHLY GROUND BLACK PEPPER	to taste

Serves 4

Preheat the oven to 190°C. Put the quartered red peppers on a baking tray, drizzle with half a tablespoon of olive oil and pop them into the oven for 20 minutes.

Meanwhile put a pot on a medium-low heat and add the remaining tablespoon of oil. Fry the onion, garlic and carrots for 5–10 minutes until they soften slightly.

Add the drained butterbeans and the roasted peppers to the pot – you can peel off the blackened skin of the peppers if you like, but I don't usually bother. Sprinkle over the rosemary and stir everything together.

Pour in 1.2 litres of boiling water, chuck in the crumbled stock cubes and bring to the boil. Turn down the heat and simmer for 20 minutes.

Blend the soup and season to taste.

September

People always come into the shop and tell us that it's soup time again – we make soup all year round but all the great produce in the shop at this time of year must inspire the customers. We have Scottish sweetcorn, local squash and pumpkins. September is also the best month to get a wide variety of British apples and pears: look out for our favourite apple varieties Delbard Estevale, Early Windsor and Zonga.

CREAMY SWEETCORN CHOWDER

This is a really good, thick soup that makes the most of fresh Scottish sweetcorn. Out of season you can use tinned sweetcorn and it will be nearly as good – just add it at the end of the cooking time and let it heat through.

OLIVE OIL OR BUTTER	1 tablespoon
LEEK	1, washed and finely chopped
FRESH SWEETCORN	2 cobs (or 1 x 340g tin, drained)
POTATOES	5 medium, peeled and diced into 2cm cubes
CARROTS	2, peeled and roughly chopped
STOCK CUBES	2
FRESH PARSLEY	a handful, very finely chopped
SALT AND FRESHLY GROUND BLACK PEPPER	to taste

Serves 4

Heat a pot on a medium-low heat and add the oil or butter.

Fry the leek gently for 10 minutes.

Using a sharp knife, slice the sweetcorn kernels off the cobs. Add the fresh corn kernels, potatoes and carrots to the pot and give it a good stir.

Pour in 1.2 litres of boiling water, throw in the crumbled stock cubes and bring to the boil. Turn down the heat and simmer for 20 minutes.

If you're using tinned sweetcorn, drain it and stir it in now and heat through for a minute.

Blend the soup until smooth and creamy and season to taste with salt and plenty of freshly ground black pepper.

Sprinkle some of the chopped parsley over each serving.

MOROCCAN BUTTERNUT SQUASH

The flavours in this soup all work really well together. If you like, the butternut squash can be replaced by sweet potato or pumpkin.

OLIVE OIL OR BUTTER	I tablespoon
ONION	I, peeled and finely chopped
FRESH GINGER	2cm, peeled and finely chopped
BUTTERNUT SQUASH	I, peeled, deseeded and roughly chopped
DRIED APRICOTS	8 dried, halved
GROUND CORIANDER	I teaspoon
GROUND CUMIN	I teaspoon
STOCK CUBES	2
SALT AND FRESHLY GROUND BLACK PEPPER	to taste

Serves 4

Heat a pot on a medium-low heat and add the oil or butter. Fry the onion and ginger for 5–10 minutes until soft.

Add the butternut squash, apricots, coriander and cumin to the pot, giving everything a stir.

Pour in 1.2 litres of boiling water, crumble in the stock cubes and bring to the boil. Turn down the heat and simmer for 15–20 minutes, until the squash is tender.

Blend the soup thoroughly to give it a really smooth texture and season to taste.

CREAMY CAULIFLOWER & COCONUT

Probably the soup we get the most good feedback on – I always imagine it's because people don't expect much from it and are more than pleasantly surprised. A cracking soup to make for guests and let them guess what's in it.

OLIVE OIL OR BUTTER	1 tablespoon
ONION	1, peeled and roughly chopped
GARLIC	2 cloves, peeled and finely chopped
CARROT	1, peeled and roughly chopped
CAULIFLOWER	1, cut into florets
STOCK CUBES	2
CREAMED COCONUT	1½ tablespoons
SALT AND FRESHLY GROUND BLACK PEPPER	to taste

Serves 4

Heat a pot on a medium-low heat and add the oil or butter. Fry the onion, garlic, carrot and cauliflower for 10 minutes until soft but not coloured.

Give everything a stir, and add 1.2 litres of boiling water, the crumbled stock cubes and the creamed coconut. Bring it all to the boil, stirring so the creamed coconut dissolves.

Turn down the heat and simmer for 15–20 minutes.

Blend thoroughly until very smooth and creamy and season well to taste.

CREAMY WOODLAND MUSHROOM

A vegan-friendly cream of mushroom soup with sweet leeks and woody thyme. All of these ingredients can grow wild in the woods, which made me think they'd work really well together in a soup.

OLIVE OIL OR BUTTER	1 tablespoon
LEEK	1, washed and finely chopped
CARROTS	2 medium, peeled and roughly chopped
GARLIC	2 cloves, peeled and finely chopped
UNSALTED CASHEWS	60g
CHESTNUT OR FIELD MUSHROOMS	350g, quartered
FRESH THYME	2 sprigs, leaves picked
STOCK CUBES	2
SALT AND FRESHLY GROUND BLACK PEPPER	to taste

Serves 4

Heat a pot on a medium-low heat and add the oil or butter. When it's hot, add the leek, carrot and garlic and fry for 5–10 minutes until they soften slightly.

Put in the cashews, mushrooms and thyme leaves and give everything a stir.

Pour in a litre of boiling water, then crumble the stock cubes into the pot and bring to the boil. Turn down the heat and simmer for 15–20 minutes.

Blend the soup until smooth and season to taste with salt and plenty of freshly ground black pepper.

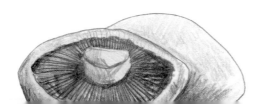

THAI SWEET POTATO

A big thanks goes to the ladies at Clementine of Broughty Ferry for a bit of help with this recipe: it wasn't quite right, and their addition of the kaffir lime leaves completed the puzzle. It's now one of our most popular soups. If you can't find kaffir lime leaves then just use a stalk of lemongrass and, either way, feel free to garnish it with some fresh coriander.

OLIVE OIL OR BUTTER	I tablespoon
ONION	I, peeled and roughly chopped
GARLIC	2 cloves, peeled and finely chopped
SWEET POTATO	I large, peeled and roughly chopped
CHILLI	I, deseeded (optional) and finely chopped
FRESH GINGER	2cm, peeled and grated
KAFFIR LIME LEAVES	I or 2
STOCK CUBES	2
CREAMED COCONUT	I½ tablespoons
SALT AND FRESHLY GROUND BLACK PEPPER	to taste

Serves 4

Heat a pot on a medium-low heat and add the oil or butter. Fry the onion and garlic for 5–10 minutes until soft.

Add the sweet potato, chilli, ginger and lime leaves and give everything a stir.

Pour in 1.2 litres of boiling water and then add the crumbled stock cubes and creamed coconut. Bring everything to the boil. Turn down the heat and simmer for 20 minutes.

Remove the lime leaf, season the soup and blend until smooth.

October

It's amazing how much of October revolves around the final day of the month and it always has a special place in our hearts because we first opened up on October 31st. Certainly the shop will be full of local pumpkins of all shapes, sizes and colours, and we also get the first of the new season Brussels sprouts and parsnips. We always wait until the first frost of the season so that the starch turns to sugar and makes them very sweet.

LENTIL SOUP

This is the first soup bag we ever sold, and it's still the most daunting. How can you tell people how to make lentil soup?! We find that grating the vegetables gives a lovely texture to the soup and saves hacking at the turnip with a sharp knife.

Feel free to add a bit of chopped bacon with the onion and celery, or why not add a teaspoon of dried chillies or cumin to spice it up a bit?

OLIVE OIL OR BUTTER	1 tablespoon
ONION	1, peeled and chopped
CELERY	1 stick, finely chopped
CARROTS	3, peeled and grated
TURNIP	1 small piece (roughly 300–400g), peeled and grated
RED LENTILS	175g, rinsed
STOCK CUBES	2
SALT AND FRESHLY GROUND BLACK PEPPER	to taste

Serves 4

Heat a pot on a medium-low heat and add the oil or butter. Fry the onion and celery for 5–10 minutes.

Add the carrots, turnip and lentils and give everything a stir.

Pour in 1.2 litres of boiling water, crumble in the stock cubes and bring to the boil. Turn down the heat and simmer for 30 minutes.

Season to taste. Delicious.

PUMPKIN & LEMONGRASS

This was inspired by a Nigel Slater recipe from the excellent book *Tender*. If you can't find pumpkin then you could substitute any kind of squash.

OLIVE OIL OR BUTTER	1 tablespoon
ONION	1, peeled and diced
CARROT	1, peeled and diced
GROUND CORIANDER	1 teaspoon
TURMERIC	1 teaspoon
LEMONGRASS	1 stalk, snapped in two and bashed a few times
PUMPKIN	1kg piece, peeled, deseeded and diced
STOCK CUBES	2
CREAMED COCONUT	1½ tablespoons

Serves 4

Heat a pot on a medium-low heat and add the oil or butter. Fry the onion, carrot, spices and lemongrass for 5–10 minutes until soft.

Add the pumpkin and continue to cook for a few minutes.

Pour in 1.2 litres of boiling water, and then throw in the crumbled stock cubes and creamed coconut, stirring until the coconut dissolves. Bring to the boil, then turn down the heat and simmer for 20 minutes.

Remove the lemongrass and blend until smooth.

PARSNIP & APPLE

The garlic-and-rosemary-infused olive oil makes this soup really special, so even if you think it sounds pointless please give it a try! It'll make the world of difference and is a neat trick to add intensified flavours when cooking.

GARLIC	2 cloves, peeled and finely chopped
ROSEMARY	2 sprigs, leaves picked off and finely chopped
OLIVE OIL	2 tablespoons
ONION	I, peeled and roughly chopped
PARSNIPS	750g, peeled and roughly chopped
APPLE	I, peeled, cored and roughly chopped
STOCK CUBES	2
SALT AND FRESHLY GROUND BLACK PEPPER	to taste

Serves 4

Put the chopped garlic and rosemary into a small bowl with the olive oil and set aside for 10 minutes to infuse.

Heat a pot on medium-low heat and add the infused oil to the pot along with the onion, parsnips and apple and fry for 10 minutes.

Pour in 1.2 litres of boiling water, chuck in the crumbled stock cubes and bring to the boil.

Turn down the heat and simmer for 20 minutes.

Blend the soup until smooth and season well to taste.

VEGGIE MULLIGATAWNY

You could add some boiled rice to this soup after it's been blended to bulk it up a bit – either way it's good.

OLIVE OIL OR BUTTER	I tablespoon
ONION	I, peeled and diced
SWEET POTATO	I, peeled and diced
CARROT	I, peeled and roughly chopped
CELERY	I stick, finely chopped
APPLE	I, peeled, cored and roughly chopped
TOMATO	I, roughly chopped
CURRY POWDER	I tablespoon
STOCK CUBES	2
SALT AND FRESHLY GROUND BLACK PEPPER	to taste

Serves 4

Heat a pot on a medium-low heat and add the oil or butter. Fry the onion, sweet potato, carrot and celery on a low heat for 10 minutes.

Add the apple, tomato and curry powder to the pot, giving everything a stir.

Pour in 1.2 litres of boiling water and the crumbled stock cubes, and then bring to the boil.

Turn down the heat and simmer gently for 20 minutes.

Blend the soup and season to taste – lots of black pepper is nice here.

November

This is the start of the really cold weather and all our customers, as if by magic or some animal instinct, are looking to load up on hearty meals to keep them cosy. A great month to get hold of all the best root vegetables and maincrop potatoes – our favourites are Maris Piper, King Edward and Desiree.

SPICY NOODLE BROTH

Try adding a couple of dashes of soy sauce and plenty of freshly ground black pepper to the finished soup.

SUNFLOWER OIL	I tablespoon
CARROT	I, peeled and very finely chopped
FRESH GINGER	thumb-sized piece, peeled and very finely chopped
GARLIC	2 cloves, peeled and finely chopped
CHILLI	I, deseeded (optional) and finely chopped
SUGAR SNAP PEAS	a handful
CHESTNUT MUSHROOMS	2 or 3, quartered
KAFFIR LIME LEAVES	2
STOCK CUBES	2
DRIED NOODLES	I nest
SPRING ONION	I, sliced

Serves 4

Heat the sunflower oil in a pot over a medium-low heat. Fry the carrot, ginger, garlic and chilli for 5–10 minutes until soft and fragrant.

Add the sugar snap peas, mushrooms and lime leaves.

Pour in 1.6 litres of boiling water, and then throw in the crumbled stock cubes and noodles. Bring everything to the boil and then reduce the heat and simmer for 5 minutes.

Scatter some sliced spring onions on each bowl and serve.

SMOKED CHILLI,
SWEET POTATO & BARLEY

The dried smoked chillies we use here have a wonderful flavour and aren't too hot. If you like you can take the chilli out at the end of cooking, discard the stalk, chop the flesh and add it back into the soup.

OLIVE OIL OR BUTTER	1 tablespoon
ONION	1, peeled and roughly chopped
CELERY	1 stick, finely chopped
SWEET POTATO	1, peeled and roughly chopped
SMOKED PAPRIKA	1 teaspoon
PEARL BARLEY	100g
SMOKED CHILLI	1 (either ancho, mulato or chipotle)
STOCK CUBES	2
SALT AND FRESHLY GROUND BLACK PEPPER	to taste

Serves 4

Heat the oil or butter in a pot on a medium-low heat. Fry the onion and celery for 5–10 minutes.

Add the sweet potato to the pot, along with the smoked paprika and barley.

Pour in 1.4 litres of boiling water, and add the crumbled stock cubes and the whole dried chilli. Bring everything to the boil. Turn down the heat and simmer for 20–30 minutes.

Season to taste and serve.

CARROT, APRICOT & GINGER

Another of the steady favourites, this is one of those flavour combos that just work. We sometimes add in a squeeze of orange or a pinch of cinnamon to give it that mulled wine flavour.

OLIVE OIL OR BUTTER	I tablespoon
ONION	I, peeled and roughly chopped
GARLIC	2 cloves, peeled and finely chopped
CARROTS	750g, peeled and roughly chopped
FRESH GINGER	thumb-sized piece, peeled and finely chopped
DRIED APRICOTS	6, roughly chopped
GROUND NUTMEG	a pinch
STOCK CUBES	2
SALT AND FRESHLY GROUND BLACK PEPPER	to taste

Serves 4

Heat a pot on a medium-low heat and add the oil or butter. Fry the onion and garlic for 5–10 minutes until soft.

Stir in the carrot, ginger, apricots and nutmeg.

Pour in 1.2 litres of boiling water and the stock cubes, and then bring to the boil. Turn down the heat and simmer for 30 minutes.

Blend the soup for a smooth texture or leave as it is, and season to taste.

BUTTERNUT SQUASH, COCONUT & APPLE

The apple in this soup acts as a sweetener and can easily be replaced by using a pear, peach or apricot.

OLIVE OIL OR BUTTER	1 tablespoon
ONION	1, peeled and roughly chopped
CARROT	1, peeled and roughly chopped
GARAM MASALA	1 teaspoon
BUTTERNUT SQUASH	1, peeled, deseeded and diced
APPLE	1, peeled, cored and roughly chopped
STOCK CUBES	2
CREAMED COCONUT	1½ tablespoons
SALT AND FRESHLY GROUND BLACK PEPPER	to taste

Serves 4

Heat a pot on a medium-low heat and add the oil or butter. Fry the onion, carrot and garam masala for 5–10 minutes.

Add the squash and apple and continue to cook for 5 minutes.

Pour in 1.2 litres of boiling water, and add the stock cubes and the creamed coconut, stirring to make sure it dissolves. Bring to the boil, then turn down the heat and simmer for 20 minutes.

Blend the soup until smooth, and then season to taste.

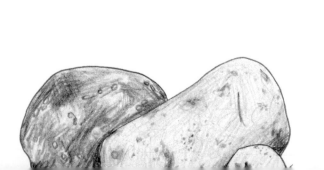

December

It's the busiest time of year for most food businesses and it seems to be all for the same produce: potatoes, carrots, parsnips, sprouts and clementines for those stockings, all in season and tasting great. It's also the best time of year to get French chestnuts for roasting or, as we've discovered, putting into soup.

SPLIT PEA, PEAR & MIXED SPICE

This was a random concoction to try and shoehorn a pear into a soup. We are so glad that it happened because it is a truly stunning soup, excellent for impressing lunch guests, and it really tastes like Christmas.

OLIVE OIL OR BUTTER	1 tablespoon
ONION	1, peeled and roughly chopped
GARLIC	2 cloves, peeled and finely chopped
PEAR	1, peeled and diced
CARROTS	2, peeled and roughly chopped
YELLOW SPLIT PEAS	150g, rinsed
MIXED SPICE	1 teaspoon
STOCK CUBES	2
SALT AND FRESHLY GROUND BLACK PEPPER	to taste

Serves 4

Heat a pot on a medium-low heat and add the oil or butter. Fry the onion and garlic for 5–10 minutes until they soften slightly.

Add the pear and carrots to the pot along with the split peas and mixed spice. Give it all a stir.

Pour in 1.3 litres of boiling water, crumble in the stock cubes, then turn up the heat and bring to the boil. Boil hard for 5 minutes and then turn the heat to low and simmer for 30 minutes more.

Blend the soup and season to taste.

TUNISIAN HOT & SMOKY VEGETABLE SOUP

Harissa is the main flavour of this mixed vegetable soup. We only use a teaspoonful but the smoked chilli paste carries so much wonderful flavour that it can turn any ordinary dish into a masterpiece.

OLIVE OIL OR BUTTER	1 tablespoon
ONION	1, peeled and finely chopped
CARROT	1 medium, peeled and roughly chopped
COURGETTE	1 medium, roughly chopped
GARLIC	2 cloves, peeled and finely chopped
SWEET POTATO	1 medium, peeled and roughly chopped
HARISSA PASTE	1 teaspoon
TOMATO PASSATA	300ml
STOCK CUBES	2
SALT AND FRESHLY GROUND BLACK PEPPER	to taste

Serves 4

Heat a pot on a medium-low heat and add the oil or butter. When it's hot, add the onion, carrot, courgette and garlic and fry for 5–10 minutes until they soften slightly.

Put in the sweet potato and harissa and give everything a stir.

Pour in 900ml of boiling water and the passata, throw the crumbled stock cubes into the pot, and bring to the boil.

Blend the soup until smooth and season to taste with salt and freshly ground black pepper.

BEETROOT, PARSNIP & HORSERADISH

This was inspired by a customer describing a soup which she'd had that was "pink, sweet and hot". We guessed it was something like beetroot mixed with parsnips, and we added the heat with horseradish root. A swirl of crème fraîche at the end will make this purple-coloured soup really attractive.

OLIVE OIL OR BUTTER	1 tablespoon
ONION	1, peeled and diced
GARLIC	1 clove, peeled and finely chopped
RAW BEETROOT	300–400g, peeled and roughly chopped
PARSNIPS	3 medium, peeled and roughly chopped
FRESH HORSERADISH	thumb-sized piece, grated
STOCK CUBES	2
SALT AND FRESHLY GROUND BLACK PEPPER	to taste

Serves 4

Heat a pot on a medium-low heat and put in the oil or butter. Fry the onion and garlic for 5–10 minutes until nice and soft.

Add the beetroot and parsnips and give everything a mix. Stir about half of the grated horseradish into the pot.

Pour in 1.2 litres of boiling water, chuck in the crumbled stock cubes, and then bring to the boil. Reduce the heat and simmer with the lid on for 25–30 minutes.

Blend everything together and season well. Then have a taste and, if you feel like you can handle more horseradish, sprinkle some more straight into your bowl.

CHESTNUT, CARROT & THYME

We tend to put this soup out at Christmas time as it works really well as a starter on the big day. It is luxurious enough but not overwhelmingly spicy or too filling. Try changing the flavours a bit by switching the carrots with parsnips and swapping the thyme with sage or rosemary.

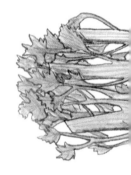

OLIVE OIL OR BUTTER	1 tablespoon
ONION	1, peeled and roughly chopped
GARLIC	2 cloves, peeled and finely chopped
CELERY	1 stick, finely chopped
VACUUM-PACKED CHESTNUTS	200g, roughly chopped
CARROTS	4, peeled and roughly chopped
THYME	a sprig, leaves only
STOCK CUBES	2
SALT AND FRESHLY GROUND BLACK PEPPER	to taste

Serves 4

Heat a pot on a medium-low heat and add the oil or butter. Fry the onion, garlic, celery, chestnuts and carrots for 10 minutes.

Sprinkle in the thyme leaves and continue to fry for another minute or so.

Add a litre of boiling water and the crumbled stock cubes, and then bring to the boil. Turn down the heat and simmer for 20 minutes.

Blend the soup 'til perfectly smooth and season to taste.

SWEET CHILLI LENTIL

A Thai-inspired twist on a traditional soup, changing the flavour dramatically by adding just a few ingredients. A great way to use up any unused root vegetables after the big day.

OLIVE OIL OR BUTTER	1 tablespoon
ONION	1, peeled and diced into 1–2cm cubes
PARSNIP	1, peeled and grated
CARROT	1, peeled and grated
GARLIC	2 cloves, peeled and finely chopped
FRESH GINGER	thumb-sized piece, peeled and grated
CHILLI	1, deseeded (optional) and finely chopped
RED LENTILS	175g, rinsed
KAFFIR LIME LEAVES	1 or 2
STOCK CUBES	2
CREAMED COCONUT	1½ tablespoons

Serves 4

Heat a pot on a medium-low heat and add the oil or butter. Fry the onion, parsnip, carrot, garlic, ginger and chilli for 10 minutes, until everything is soft but not coloured.

Add the lentils and lime leaves and give it all a stir.

Pour in 1.2 litres of boiling water, and add the crumbled stock cubes and the creamed coconut, stirring to make sure it dissolves. Turn down the heat and simmer for 15–20 minutes.

Blend the soup 'til smooth or eat as it is – either way it's great!

INDEX